SCIENCE EXPLORER

UNEARTHING

FOSSILS

Follow the Clues

by Tamra B. Orr

CHERRY LAKE PUBLISHING · ANN ARBOR, MICHIGAN

This book is intended to introduce readers to the Next Generation Science Standards (NGSS). These standards emphasize a general set of eight practices for scientific investigation, rather than a rigid set of steps. Keywords taken from the NGSS are highlighted in the text. The eight science practices are:

1. Asking questions
2. Developing and using models
3. Planning and carrying out investigations
4. Analyzing and interpreting data
5. Using mathematics and computational thinking
6. Constructing explanations
7. Engaging in argument from evidence
8. Obtaining, evaluating, and communicating information

Published in the United States of America by Cherry Lake Publishing
Ann Arbor, Michigan
www.cherrylakepublishing.com

CONTENT EDITOR: Melissa Miller, Next Generation Science Standards Writer, Science Teacher, Farmington, Arkansas
READING ADVISOR: Marla Conn, ReadAbility, Inc.
BOOK DESIGN AND ILLUSTRATION: The Design Lab

PHOTO CREDITS: Cover and page 1, ©Marcio Jose Bastos Silva/Shutterstock, Inc.; page 4, Long Zheng / http://www.flickr.com / CC BY-SA 2.0; page 5, ©All Canada Photos/Alamy; page 6, © Caro/Alamy; page 7, ©Buddy Mays/Alamy; page 9, ©AP Photo/Paul Sakuma; page 10, ©Briancweed/Dreamstime.com; page 11, ©Artush/ Shutterstock, Inc.; page 12, ©Mega Pixel/Shutterstock, Inc.; page 13, ©Markus Mainka/Shutterstock, Inc.; page 14, ©National Geographic Image Collection/ Alamy; page 15, ©Ozja/Shutterstock, Inc.; page 16, ©Natursports/Dreamstime. com; page 17, ©ZUMA Press, Inc./Alamy; page 18, ©Anneka/Shutterstock, Inc.; page 20, ©Pressmaster/Shutterstock, Inc.; page 21, ©AP Photo/The Tri-City Herald, Richard Dickin; page 22, ©AP Photo/M. Spencer Green; page 23, ©Catalin Petolea/ Shutterstock, Inc.; page 24, ©Littleny/Dreamstime.com; page 25, ©Blend Images/ Alamy; page 26, ©Robert Landau/Alamy; page 27, ©Vladislav Gajic/Shutterstock, Inc.; page 28, ©Kevin Schafer/Alamy; page 29, ©OJO Images Ltd/Alamy.

LIBRARY OF CONGRESS CATALOGING-IN-PUBLICATION DATA
Orr, Tamra, author.
Unearthing fossils / by Tamra B. Orr.
pages cm. — (Science explorer) (Follow the clues)
Summary: "Use the Next Generation Science Standards to identify the fossils of an ancient mammoth." — Provided by publisher.
Audience: Grades 4 to 6.
Includes bibliographical references and index.
ISBN 978-1-62431-781-1 (lib. bdg.) — ISBN 978-1-62431-791-0 (pbk.) — ISBN 978-1-62431-801-6 (pdf) — ISBN 978-1-62431-811-5 (ebook)
 1. Mammoths—Juvenile literature. 2. Fossils—Juvenile literature.
3. Geochronometry—Juvenile literature. I. Title.

QE882.P8077 2014
569.67—dc23   2013045292

Cherry Lake Publishing would like to acknowledge the work of The Partnership for 21st Century Skills.
Please visit www.p21.org for more information.

Printed in the United States of America, Corporate Graphics Inc.
January 2014

TABLE OF CONTENTS

CHAPTER 1

AN ANCIENT ANIMAL

Zed and the remains of several other animals have been found at the La Brea Tar Pits in Los Angeles, California.

"Did you know that Zed's tusks were more than 3 feet long?" Veronica Marshall asked her brother, Jordan. He rolled his eyes but did not reply. He just kept setting the table for dinner.

"They think he was more than 40 years old when he died," added Veronica, grabbing silverware out of the drawer. Once again, there was no reply from Jordan. He had heard all of this a million times before.

Veronica had talked of nothing but Zed since their dad had told them about the massive creature. Zed had been discovered in Los Angeles, California, in 2009. Why Veronica was so fascinated by the bones of a mammoth that had been **extinct** for thousands of years mystified Jordan. What was so exciting about a bunch of old bones anyway? At the museum, they'd seen lots of bones of creatures that had been extinct for thousands of years.

"Dad said that the bones were in almost perfect condition," she continued. "Don't you love the fact that they called him Zed? Isn't it amazing that we have a **paleontologist** for a dad?"

Paleontologists study a variety of animals, from dinosaurs and fish to birds and mammals.

Jordan paused and then grinned. His sister did have a good point. Having a father who spent his life digging up bones and studying them was pretty cool. The days that he and Veronica got to go to the museum and help him were even better.

The next day, Dr. Marshall brought Veronica and Jordan with him to the museum. "It's an exciting day," he told them. "We have a new mammoth fossil to examine. It was just unearthed last week."

"Do you think it could be a part of Zed's skeleton?" Veronica asked.

"Hmm," Dr. Marshall replied. "Good question. I suppose that is possible. It was discovered in the same area as Zed's other bones. We'll need to gather more information, though. Why don't we take a closer look and see what we can find out?"

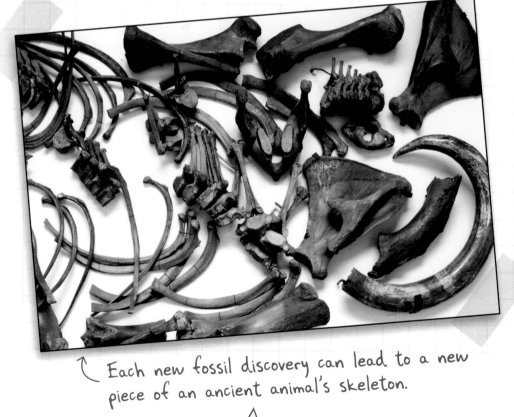

Each new fossil discovery can lead to a new piece of an ancient animal's skeleton.

Jordan and Veronica were excited to find out if the new fossil was part of Zed.

"How will we be able to tell if the fossil belongs to Zed?" Jordan asked. A puzzled expression crept across his face.

"Well, we know which fossils are definitely Zed's," Dr. Marshall answered.

Jordan and Veronica smiled as they realized what their dad was getting at. "We can compare the old fossils to the new one!" Jordan exclaimed.

Finding fossils, digging them up, and getting them back to a laboratory or museum undamaged takes a lot of hard work and planning. A successful dig is worth the effort, though. It can allow researchers to gather a great deal of information about prehistoric times.

Paleontologists begin by searching for areas where ancient **sedimentary** rock layers are exposed. Once they are at a dig site, paleontologists work carefully, digging through small areas, one at a time, to avoid damaging any fossils. When a fossil is found, they do not dig it up immediately. They photograph the area, mark map locations, and take rock and soil samples from the area around the fossil. This will provide important background information to help the paleontologists identify the fossil and learn more about the past.

Digging a fossil out of the ground is a risky and delicate process. Most of the time, paleontologists prefer to cut out a large chunk of rock surrounding the fossil and send the whole thing to a laboratory. There, they can more carefully take out the fossil, reducing the risk of damaging it. Paleontologists use small tools such as brushes and picks to slowly remove the dirt and rock from around the fossil. They sometimes spray water onto the rock to soften it. With hard work, enough time, and a little luck, they can end up with a clean, unbroken fossil.

CHAPTER 2

TAKING A CLOSER LOOK

Paleontologists work slowly and carefully to avoid damaging delicate fossils.

Dr. Marshall pulled back a sheet that was covering a long metal table. Underneath it was a huge gray fossil with a thin, curved shape. "Be careful," Dr. Marshall warned. "We don't want to damage it."

Veronica and Jordan looked at the fossil with amazement. "We're going to need a plan if we want to solve this mystery," said Veronica.

"I think the first thing we need to do is figure out what kind of bone it is," Jordan suggested.

↑ Rib bones have a long, narrow, curved shape.

"Then we can compare it to the bones on Zed's body to see if it's similar," added Veronica.

"Those are great ideas," Dr. Marshall said. "But don't forget that the fossil might not be a part of Zed's skeleton. You should also compare it to Martha, another partial mammoth skeleton that was found in the same area."

Dr. Marshall led Veronica and Jordan to see Zed and Martha. The kids examined the two mammoth skeletons closely. "What kind of bone do you think the new fossil is?" Jordan asked Veronica.

"It has to be a rib," she said, pointing at Zed's skeleton. "No other bone is shaped like that."

"You're exactly right," said Dr. Marshall. "The new fossil is part of a mammoth rib cage."

"How should we compare these ribs to the new one?" Veronica asked.

"Why not measure their sizes?" Jordan suggested. "We can make a chart to keep track of our measurements." After getting a notebook and pen from Dr. Marshall's office, he drew the following chart:

	Rib length	Rib thickness
Zed		
Martha		
New fossil		

Jordan drew a chart to help keep track of the fossil measurements.

Veronica reviewed her brother's chart carefully. "This looks great," she said. "But how will we measure the thickness? We can't stick a ruler through the middle of the bone!"

"Why not measure the **circumference** of the bones?" Dr. Marshall proposed. "You can wrap a tape measure around the fossil to get your measurement."

"Great idea, Dad!" Jordan exclaimed. "Let's start measuring!"

Jordan and Veronica carefully measured rib bones from the skeletons of Zed and Martha. They measured each one twice to be sure they had the numbers right. Then they wrote down the longest rib

Careful measurements are an important part of many scientific investigations.

Veronica knew that measurements alone wouldn't be enough to identify the new fossil.

↳

	Longest rib length	Rib circumference
Zed	48 inches	6.25 inches
Martha	40 inches	5.75 inches
New fossil	42 inches	5.75 inches

measurement in the notebook. Once they had the **data** they needed, they went to measure the new fossil as well.

Veronica scratched her head as she looked at the chart. "It's not quite as long as Zed's longest rib, but it is a little longer than Martha's longest rib."

"It has the same circumference as Martha's rib," Jordan added.

"So which one does it belong to?" Veronica asked.

"It looks like we need to gather some more information," Dr. Marshall said.

In prehistoric times, there were no historians or scientists around to study the world and record information. So fossils are one of the only ways that today's researchers can learn about ancient times. Sometimes a single fossil discovery can completely change the way we think about the past.

In 1924, paleontologists discovered a new dinosaur. Its fossilized body was found atop fossilized eggs that were believed to belong to a different dinosaur species. The scientists believed that the newly discovered dinosaur had been attempting to steal and eat the eggs, when it died. They named it Oviraptor, which means "egg thief."

Decades later, more Oviraptor remains were found atop piles of fossilized eggs. However, the new fossils were revealed to be Oviraptor eggs. The dinosaur was not stealing eggs. It was sitting on its own nest! This discovery showed Oviraptor's name to be inaccurate. Paleontology is an ever-changing field, and we still have a lot to learn about the ancient past.

CHAPTER 3

OLD BONES

↰ Mammoths lived tens of thousands of years ago.

"What other information could we use to compare these fossils?" Jordan asked. Veronica scratched her head and wrinkled her brow in concentration.

"Well, Zed died around 50,000 years ago," said Dr. Marshall, "and Martha's skeleton is much newer. She died around 20,000 years ago."

Veronica's face lit up. "If there was a way to figure out how old the new fossil is, we could see if it was the same age as Zed or Martha."

"How could we do that?" asked Jordan.

"First, I'll need to talk to the paleontologists who dug up the fossil so we can get more information about the rocks it was buried in," said Dr. Marshall. "Then I can show you how to use that information to calculate the fossil's age. We do it all the time here at the museum."

"Awesome!" Jordan shouted. "Let's do it now!"

Dr. Marshall grinned. "Slow down, buddy. It will take a day or so for me to get the information first."

The next day, Jordan and Veronica returned to the museum with their dad. Dr. Marshall explained that paleontologists can tell roughly

The depth where a fossil is discovered can provide important information about its age.

↳ Paleontologists keep careful notes and records as they dig up fossils.

how old a fossil is by studying the layers of rock where it is found. The deeper a rock layer is below the surface, the older it usually is.

"But how do you know how old each rock layer is?" Jordan asked.

"It can be tough to figure out exactly," Dr. Marshall agreed. "This method does not tell us exactly how many years something has been buried. Instead, it tells us how old one fossil is compared to another."

"Got it," said Veronica. "So how deep was our fossil?"

"And how deep were Zed and Martha?" asked Jordan.

Dr. Marshall wrote down the three depths and labeled them *ZED*, *MARTHA*, and *NEW FOSSIL*. "As you can see, the new fossil was found

Always be extremely careful when you are entering numbers into a calculator.

about 15 feet underground. Most of Zed was found about 30 feet underground, and Martha was at about 12 feet. You can calculate which one it is closer to by subtracting the numbers."

Jordan and Veronica entered the numbers into their calculator. As they wrote down their answers, Dr. Marshall gave them some extra advice. "Be sure to double-check your results to make sure you have it right," he said.

"We did!" said Veronica excitedly. "The new fossil was located just three feet beneath the depth where Martha's other bones were discovered."

"And it is 15 feet above where Zed was found," Jordan added. "Now that's an important clue!"

RUNNING THE NUMBERS

Math calculations in science experiments must be as precise as possible to be effective. Even a small math error can cause you to have very different results when you reach the experiment's conclusion. Here are some tips you can follow to be sure you end up with the right data:

☆ Double-check your work: If you do a math problem two times and get two different answers, you will know that one of them is wrong. Keep trying until you get the same answer multiple times.

☆ Check your work with a calculator: Doing calculations by hand or in your head is a good way to become better at math. However, a calculator can help you make sure you are getting the right results.

☆ Avoid rounding up or down as much as possible: If you are working with decimals, try not to round up or down unless you need to. Even these tiny changes can have an effect on your final results, especially if you are working with small numbers.

☆ Record your calculations carefully: Write down each step of your work as you go. Go slowly and use your best handwriting. This will make it easier to look back through your work if you determine later on that you have made a mistake.

CHAPTER 4

PUTTING IT ALL TOGETHER

Thinking about how different pieces of data go together can help you draw conclusions about your original question.

Jordan and Veronica looked back at their charts and calculations. "Now what do we do?" asked Jordan.

"I think we have enough information now to figure out the answer!" Veronica said happily.

"I think you're right," said Dr. Marshall. "You just need to analyze your data and come up with an explanation."

"First, let's look at the measurements we took," Jordan said.

Veronica ran her finger along the lines of the chart as she read. "The new fossil is a lot closer in size to Martha's rib than it is to Zed's rib," she said.

"It's not exactly the same, though," Jordan added.

"That's true," she replied, "but look at the ages of the fossils."

"The new fossil was only a little deeper underground than Martha's other bones," Jordan said.

"Dad, do you think they might be close enough together to be part of the same skeleton?" asked Veronica.

Dr. Marshall nodded thoughtfully. "It could be," he said. "Sometimes fossils from slightly different depths can actually come from the same time period."

↑ Sometimes many fossils are found right next to each other.

Veronica looked at Jordan with a huge smile on her face. "I think we might have solved the mystery!"

"Do you think the new fossil might really belong to Martha?" Jordan asked. "That's so cool!"

"I was really hoping it would be a part of Zed," Veronica said. "But this is still really amazing!"

"We can't be 100 percent sure until I do some more tests with the other paleontologists," Dr. Marshall said. "But you guys might just be on to something. How would you like to present your findings to the other experts here at the museum?"

Dr. Marshall had barely gotten the words out of his mouth before Jordan and Veronica shouted at the same time, "Yes!"

↑ Veronica and Jordan hoped to impress the expert paleontologists at their dad's museum.

UNEXPECTED RESULTS

Science experiments can often result in answers that are very different from your original predictions. Sometimes they might prove the opposite idea that you thought they would. Other times, they might not answer your question at all. Don't get discouraged if this happens to you. Science is not about proving yourself right or wrong. It is about solving the world's many mysteries and finding accurate explanations for why things work the way they do. Even an experiment that doesn't answer your original question might provide you with enough information to plan a new investigation.

CHAPTER 5

SPREADING THE WORD

⤷ Posters are a great way to share visual information with an audience.

Back at home that night, Veronica and Jordan began preparing to present their findings to the museum's paleontologists the next day. "Let's make posters to show what we learned about the fossil," Jordan suggested.

"That's a great idea," Veronica agreed. She and Jordan gathered their supplies and got to work.

The next morning, they put their posters on display around the fossil, and Dr. Marshall and his fellow paleontologists gathered around them.

"So what can you tell us about this fossil?" one of the paleontologists asked.

It is important to speak clearly when presenting your findings.

"A lot!" said Veronica. She and Jordan began to explain why they thought the fossil might be a part of one of the museum's mammoth skeletons. "First, we looked at the fossil's shape to figure out what kind of bone it is."

Jordan pointed to a drawing of the fossil. "Because of the long, curved shape, we determined that it is a rib."

"Then we measured the rib and compared it to measurements of Zed's ribs and Martha's ribs," Veronica continued.

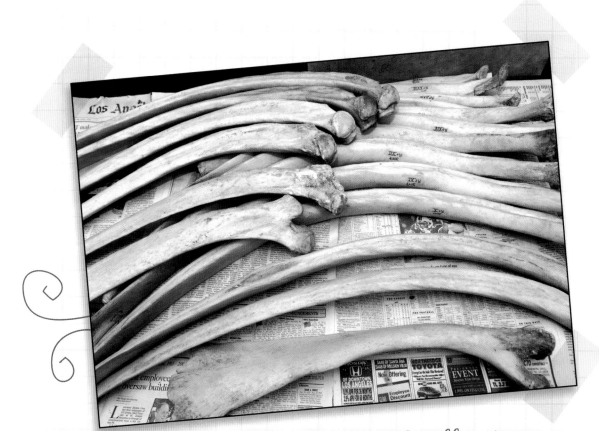

Paleontologists can often identify different bones based on their shape and size.

Mammoth bones are huge!

"It didn't match either one exactly, but it was close to Martha's size," Jordan said. He showed the group a poster with the measurement chart on it.

"Very interesting," said one of the paleontologists. Jordan looked at Veronica and smiled.

"Finally," said Veronica, "we used the age of the rocks that the fossil was buried in to figure out how old the fossil is." She pointed at a poster showing their math calculations.

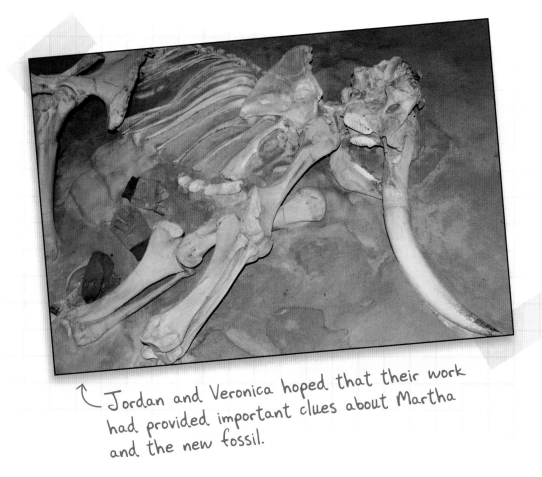

Jordan and Veronica hoped that their work had provided important clues about Martha and the new fossil.

"It is about the same age as Martha," Jordan explained. "Based on the age and the measurements, we think this fossil might belong to Martha's skeleton."

The paleontologists clapped in approval. "This is fantastic work," one of them said. "We'll have to do some more tests to make sure, but your theory could be right!"

Jordan and Veronica were both grinning from ear to ear. They couldn't believe that they had helped solve a scientific mystery.

"Next thing we know, you'll be discovering a new dinosaur!" Dr. Marshall said as he looked at Jordan and Veronica with pride.

"Maybe they'll call it Marshall, " Jordan added with a grin.

One of the most important steps of any scientific investigation is sharing your findings with others. Everyone from your fellow scientists to your friends and neighbors will be interested in hearing about your discoveries. Some scientists might use your findings in their own investigations. Other people might just be curious to find out about the latest scientific developments.

When you are presenting information, carefully consider who your audience will be. If you are sharing with other scientists, you might write a detailed paper filled with charts, numbers, and science terms. Your fellow scientists will want as much information as possible, and they will know what difficult science words mean.

When you are sharing with people who aren't science experts, you should take a different approach. Be sure to explain everything as simply and clearly as possible. Include any background information that the audience might need. Avoid using complicated science words or including details that people might find confusing. Imagine that you don't know anything about your topic. What questions would you have? Include the answers to these questions in your report.

GLOSSARY

circumference (sur-KUHM-fur-uhns) the distance around something

data (DAY-tuh) information collected in a place so that something can be done with it

extinct (ik-STINGKT) no longer found alive; known about only through fossils or history

paleontologist (pay-lee-uhn-TAHL-uh-jist) a scientist who studies fossils and other ancient life-forms

sedimentary (sed-uh-MEN-tur-ee) rock that is formed by layers of sediment that have been pressed together

FOR MORE INFORMATION

BOOKS

Arato, Rona. *Fossils: Clues to Ancient Life*. New York: Crabtree
    Publishing, 2004.

Morgan, Ben, and Douglas Palmer. *Rock and Fossil Hunter*. New York: DK
    Publishing, 2005.

Pellant, Chris. *Rocks and Fossils*. New York: Kingfisher, 2011.

Squire, Ann O. *Fossils*. New York: Children's Press, 2012.

WEB SITES

Life of a Vertebrate Fossil

www.paleobiology.si.edu/LVF/

Follow paleontologists as they study a vertebrate fossil.

PaleontOLogy: The Big Dig

www.amnh.org/explore/ology/paleontology

Test your fossil knowledge, read interviews with paleontologists, and
explore online activities.

INDEX

ABOUT THE AUTHOR

Tamra B. Orr is an author living in the Pacific Northwest. Orr has a degree in Secondary Education and English from Ball State University. She is the mother to four, and the author of more than 350 books for readers of all ages. When she isn't writing or reading books, she is writing letters to friends all over the world. Although fascinated by all aspects of science, most of her current scientific method skills are put to use tracking down lost socks, missing keys, and overdue library books.